WEATHER MAKES THEM SLEEP

BLACK BEAR HIBERNATION

by Martha London

Consultant: Beth Gambro
Reading Specialist, Yorkville, Illinois

Bearport Publishing

Minneapolis, Minnesota

Teaching Tips

Before Reading

- Look at the cover of the book. Discuss the picture and the title.
- Ask readers to brainstorm a list of what they already know about black bears. What can they expect to see in this book?
- Go on a picture walk, looking through the pictures to discuss vocabulary and make predictions about the text.

During Reading

- Read for purpose. Encourage readers to think about black bear hibernation as they are reading.
- Ask readers to look for the details of the book. What do black bears do to get ready to hibernate?
- If readers encounter an unknown word, ask them to look at the sounds in the word. Then, ask them to look at the rest of the page. Are there any clues to help them understand?

After Reading

- Encourage readers to pick a buddy and reread the book together.
- Ask readers to name one reason black bears sleep. Find the page that tells about this thing.
- Ask readers to write or draw something they learned about black bear hibernation.

Credits:
Cover and title page, © TangoFoxtrot2018/Shutterstock; 3, © Svetlana Foote/Shutterstock; 5, © Glass and Nature/Shutterstock; 7TL, © Sean Xu/Shutterstock; 7TR, © RomanKhomlyak/iStock; 7BL, © BRUCE/Adobe Stock; 7BR, © cweimer4/iStock; 8-9, © Jillian Cooper/iStock; 10-11, © Jason/Adobe Stock; 12-13, © Ipsimus/Adobe Stock; 15, © Manuel Lacoste/Shutterstock; 16-17, © Nature Picture Library / Alamy Stock Photo/Alamy; 18-19, © All Canada Photos / Alamy Stock Photo/Alamy; 21, © Seth Schneider/iStock; 22T, © Betty4240/iStock; 22ML, © Chris Desborough/Shutterstock; 22MR, © hkuchera/Adobe Stock; 22B, © Robert S. Michelson/Tom Stack & Assoc. / Alamy Stock Photo/Alamy; 23TL, © hkuchera/Adobe Stock; 23TM, © mirceax/iStock; 23TR, © staticnak1983/iStock; 23BL, © Erik Agar/Shutterstock; 23BR, © Brisana/iStock.

STATEMENT ON USAGE OF GENERATIVE ARTIFICIAL INTELLIGENCE
Bearport Publishing remains committed to publishing high-quality nonfiction books. Therefore, we restrict the use of generative AI to ensure accuracy of all text and visual components pertaining to a book's subject. See BearportPublishing.com for details.

Library of Congress Cataloging-in-Publication Data

Names: London, Martha, author. | Gambro, Beth, consultant.
Title: Black bear hibernation / by Martha London ; consultant Beth Gambro,
   Reading Specialist.
Description: Minneapolis, Minnesota : Bearport Publishing Company, [2024] |
   Series: Weather makes them sleep | Includes bibliographical references
   and index.
Identifiers: LCCN 2023028915 (print) | LCCN 2023028916 (ebook) | ISBN
   9798889162223 (library binding) | ISBN 9798889162278 (paperback) | ISBN
   9798889162315 (ebook)
Subjects: LCSH: Black bear--Juvenile literature. | Black
   bear--Hibernation--Juvenile literature.
Classification: LCC QL737.C27 L66 2024 (print) | LCC QL737.C27 (ebook) |
   DDC 599.78/51565--dc23/eng/20230712
LC record available at https://lccn.loc.gov/2023028915
LC ebook record available at https://lccn.loc.gov/2023028916

Copyright © 2024 Bearport Publishing Company. All rights reserved. No part of this publication may be reproduced in whole or in part, stored in any retrieval system, or transmitted in any form or by any means, electronic, mechanical, photocopying, recording, or otherwise, without written permission from the publisher.

For more information, write to Bearport Publishing, 5357 Penn Avenue South, Minneapolis, MN 55419.

Contents

Cozy Up 4

Eat, Sleep, Repeat 22

Glossary 23

Index 24

Read More 24

Learn More Online 24

About the Author 24

Cozy Up

It is getting cold outside!

A black bear is busy making its **den**.

What is the bear getting ready for?

5

Most black bears live in places with four **seasons**.

These seasons have different weather.

Some are warmer.

Others are colder.

It is hot in the summer.

There is plenty of food.

Black bears munch on berries and **insects**.

Bears eat a lot during the summer.

They need to get food while they can.

Soon, the weather gets colder.

There is less food for the bears.

In the fall, black bears make dens.

Some make these cozy homes in caves.

Others dig holes in the ground.

They fill their dens with leaves.

The weather is cold in the winter.

Black bears head into their dens.

They go to sleep.

Dens keep the bears warm while they snooze.

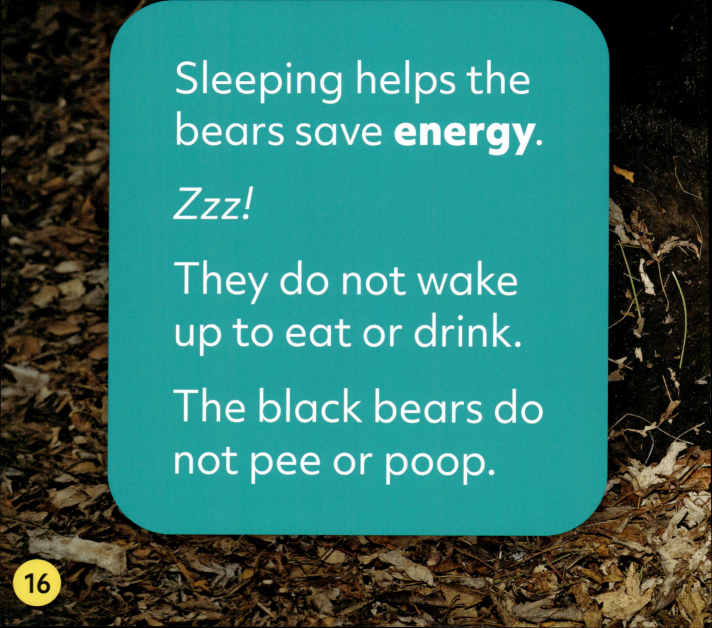

Sleeping helps the bears save **energy**.

Zzz!

They do not wake up to eat or drink.

The black bears do not pee or poop.

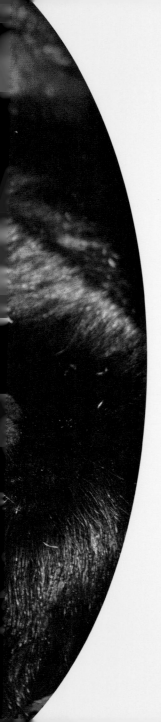

Mother bears even sleep when they have **cubs**!

The baby bears drink milk from their mother's body.

They get bigger as their mother sleeps.

Soon, the season changes again.

The weather gets warmer in the spring.

Plants begin to grow.

It is time for black bears to get up!

Eat, Sleep, Repeat

Glossary

cubs baby bears

den a hidden place where an animal sleeps and has babies

energy the power needed by all living things to be active and stay alive

insects small animals with three body parts and six legs

seasons the parts of the year with different weather

Index

cubs 19
den 4, 12, 14, 22
food 8, 10, 22
season 6, 20
sleep 14, 16, 19, 22
weather 6, 10, 14, 20

Read More

Albertson, Al. *Black Bears (Animals of the Forest).* Minneapolis: Bellwether Media, Inc., 2020.

McDowell, Pamela. *Black Bear (Backyard Animals).* New York: Lightbox Learning Inc., 2022.

Learn More Online

1. Go to **www.factsurfer.com** or scan the QR code below.
2. Enter **"Black Bear Hibernation"** into the search box.
3. Click on the cover of this book to see a list of websites.

About the Author

Martha London loves writing about animals! She has two cats. They love to sleep in the sun.